The Best
Is
Yet to Be

by
Kurt Rommel

translated and adapted by
David L. Scheidt

Fortress Press
Philadelphia

This book is a freely adapted translation of *Das Alter—die hohe Zeit des Lebens,* copyright © 1973 by Quell Verlag in Stuttgart, Germany.

Biblical quotations from the Revised Standard Version of the Bible, copyrighted 1946 and 1952 by the Division of Christian Education of the National Council of the Churches of Christ in the United States of America, are used by permission.

The cover photograph is by H. Armstrong Roberts. Photographs on pp. 10 and 34–35 are by George B. Ammon; on pp. 25, 33, 39, and 79 by Harold M. Lambert; on pp. 30, 40, 56–57, 63, 66, and 68 by H. Armstrong Roberts; and on pp. 13, 14, 16–17, 20, 23, 27, 43, 46, 49, 51, 52, 60, 70–72, and 76 by Wallowitch.

Library of Congress Catalog Card Number 74-26327

ISBN 0-8006-1096-2

4659L74   *Printed in U.S.A.*   1–1096

The Best Is Yet to Be

Contents

Looking Forward

Almost everyone looks forward to living to a ripe old age. But no one wants to be old. In fact, we even avoid the word old. We use other words and expressions which sound less harsh and threatening. We prefer to say that we are getting on in years.

However we say it, the truth is that more and more of us are living to a ripe old age. More and more of us are growing older. We are getting on in years.

The purpose of this book is to share with the reader some thoughts, some reflections, on what it means to get on in years. These reflections are not scientific or theoretical essays. Nor is the order in which they are presented particularly systematic. On the contrary, they are a random collection. And they are intensely practical. They grow out of the experience of real men and women who are getting on in years.

If there is any moral or conclusion to be drawn from the reflections offered here, it is this: getting on in years can be the most wonderful experience of our lives. These years, so often and so rightly called the "golden years," are a gift of God's love and grace. They are not a downhill retreat, but the attainment of that crowning peak of life to which the poet so thrillingly invites us:

> Grow old along with me!
> The best is yet to be,
> The last of life, for which the first was made.
>   —Robert Browning, *Rabbi ben Ezra*

Kurt Rommel

The Best Is Yet to Be

Getting On in Years

't something that happens
irthday, or when the time
ething that has been going
s. It is a part of life. It *is* life.
rer, when we become very
g on in years, that we are

? Indeed not! Getting on in
iges. It affords opportunities
younger years.
)on't regret it. Don't lament
as a gracious gift from God.

r the gift of getting on in
the years that lie behind
and opportunities that lie
ik forward to what is yet

I have been young, and now am old;
yet I have not seen the righteous forsaken.

Psalm 37:25

Seeing Our Children as Adults

Getting on in years gives us the opportunity to see our children as adults, and at the same time to understand ourselves a little better.

Our grown-up children certainly do things differently than we did. They are much more free and open than we were. They have more leisure, more money, more conveniences, more of everything than we had. And it seems that they are always looking for more.

But let's be honest. If we had it all to do over again, if we were now in their situation, wouldn't we be doing as they do? After all, the times have changed and we must change with them.

The best way to bridge the generation gap is to recognize that our children must live their own lives in their day and in their own way. Certainly we can offer advice. But advice is one thing—meddling is another. We have to recognize the difference and act accordingly.

Lord, I thank you for my children. They do things so differently from what I did. But don't let that alienate us from each other. Give me strength to let them live their own lives and to avoid meddling in their affairs.

When I was a child, I spoke like a child, I thought like a child, I reasoned like a child; when I became a man, I gave up childish ways.

1 Corinthians 13:11

Grandchildren

and Change

It's wonderful to have grandchildren. We're proud of them. We love them.

But oh, how we complain about them. They are brought up differently than we were brought up. Discipline seems foreign to their experience. They get away with entirely too much. They don't appreciate anything. They have too much.

At least that's the way it seems to us. And that could be a sign that we are getting on in years, that we need to adjust our thinking, that we need to look at things differently.

Of course we are growing older, but that doesn't mean that we cannot change our views or accept different ways. Getting on in years gives us a new choice of views.

Dear God, it's wonderful to have grandchildren Help me to realize though, that they are not mine to bring up, but that they can help me to grow and change even as I see them grow and change.

Grandchildren are the crown of the aged.

Proverbs 17:6

Young and Old Together

They call this the "century of youth." And for good reason: everything in our society accentuates being young, everything seems geared to youth. At times, we who are getting on in years feel "left out."

But the young grow older too. Before this century is over it may well be called the "geriatric era."

Much rivalry between the generations is foolish. The young need to recognize that we who are getting on in years are not decrepit, useless, mentally unglued. And we who are getting on in years need to recognize that those whose youth we envy—we do envy them, don't we?—are not all that far behind us.

They are our past. We are their future. We need each other. In each other we see the past and the future together.

> It's great, Lord, to be young. But I am not sorry that I am getting on in years. Help the generations to recognize that we need each other. Help us to stay on speaking terms with each other, and to remain friends.

For the body does not consist of one member but of many. . . . If the whole body were an eye, where would be the hearing? . . . But as it is, God arranged . . . each one of them, as he chose.

1 Corinthians 12:14-18

A Time to Say No

"What do the old folks know?"

"They aren't with it anymore."

"They live in the past."

That's what many of the young folks say. And if they don't say it, they think it.

Ah, but when they need a baby-sitter, someone to take care of the children for an evening, a weekend, a vacation! That's an entirely different story. We're good enough for that!

We resent the imposition, don't we? Yet invariably we suppress the resentment and say yes. We feel we have to say yes. Somehow, it would be immoral for us to say no.

We need to face up to the fact that there are times when we ought to say no. Not because we want to

assert our independence or express our resentment at being taken for granted. We need to say no because we are getting on in years. We can't do what we used to do the way we used to do it. We can't take as much excitement. We need our rest.

Of course we want to help our children, when they need us. We are more than glad to take care of the grandchildren from time to time. But there are times when we need to say no and mean it.

> Lord, I want to be a help to my family, not a burden. But I need my rest. I can't do what I used to do. Help me, Lord, to do what I can. Help me to say no when I should.

Jesus said to them, "Come away by yourselves . . . and rest a while." For many were coming and going, and they had no leisure even to eat.

Mark 6:31

Seeing Clearly

Getting on in years has some definite advantages. One of them is the realization that we have more years behind us than we have ahead of us.

What kind of advantage is that? Let's look at it this way: When we were young time meant nothing to us. We had the rest of our life ahead of us.

Now we have most of our life behind us. At our stage in life, time is a very precious commodity—too precious to squander or waste. We are more careful how we spend the time that is left to us.

We learn to recognize what is really important in life and what is not. Things which once annoyed or worried us, which caused us to lose our temper or emotional balance, no longer hold sway over us. Their control over us is broken.

At least now we can see things more nearly as they really are; we can take things more easily in stride. Best of all, we can smile—even laugh—more readily and more frequently.

> Lord, now at last I see more clearly what is important in life and what is not. And because I see this, many a burden is lifted from my mind and heart, and I can smile and laugh. Thank you for this gift.

So teach us to number our days that we may get a heart of wisdom.

Psalm 90:12

Running Errands

Retirement! Free at least from the daily grind and pressure.

But what does one do now? Many a man finds himself at sixes and sevens. He's at a loss to occupy himself. So his wife, who has her daily routine, lets him take over the errands, especially the shopping chores that are a nuisance to her.

He does them. But he's not very happy about them. Running errands is demeaning for one who is getting on in years.

Really? Going to the store can be quite an opportunity. Comparing prices offers an education in economics. You can meet friends and neighbors along the way and not just pass the time of day with a nod of the head or a wave of the hand. You have a real opportunity to collect the news of the day that never gets into print.

But more important, you can get to know your neighbors from an entirely different perspective.

There is much to be said for running errands when one gets on in years. The human contacts, the chats and banter along the way are refreshing and renewing.

And besides, you really are helping your wife.

> Lord, help me to see the chores of the day as opportunities that are beneficial to me and helpful to the one I love.

He who loves his wife loves himself.

Ephesians 5:28

Crossing Streets

Who would ever think that crossing the street would be a problem? But it is when you are getting on in years. Traffic is so much heavier today than formerly. And faster—much faster.

Where do all the cars and trucks come from? Where are they hurrying? Why the hurry?

Our reflexes aren't what they used to be. Neither is our vision. Our step isn't as quick. We have too much on our minds. We don't pay attention to the traffic signals.

Drivers have a lot on their minds too. They aren't always alert and as sharp as they should be. It isn't easy for them to see us when we walk out from between parked cars or try to cross the street in the middle of the block. Nor can they anticipate that we will try to cross against the light.

As we grow older, we need to be more careful. We need to obey the traffic rules as conscientiously as we expect the drivers to obey them. And we should not be too proud to ask for or accept assistance from another street crosser.

> Lord, the traffic terrifies me. I get confused. Help the drivers to be careful. Help me to be careful.

The Lord will be your confidence and will keep your foot from being caught.

Proverbs 3:26

Time to Catch Up

Getting on in years affords the opportunity to do many things for which we never had the time. Now there is plenty of time.

There are books we have always wanted to read. There are places we have wanted to visit. Not faraway places, but places here at home, close by. There is so much we want to learn, so much we want to catch up on in the world: food and energy problems, developments in the world community, preserving the environment, the quest for peace.

Now at last we have the time. And we have the means.

Radio and television bring the world right into our living rooms. Newspapers, magazines, books, lectures—even college courses—on every conceivable theme and subject are accessible to us.

But we need to catch up on other things as well, the noble things that speak to the soul and spirit, the things that edify and uplift or challenge and inform.

We need also to catch up on the little things of life: children at play, waves that lap against the shore, and the sounds and peace of the evening hours.

> Lord, I do not want to be a relic. I want to catch up and keep up with what is going on in the world. But I want to see and enjoy the silent beauties that uplift the heart and cheer the spirit.

I will meditate on all thy work,
and muse on thy mighty deeds.

Psalm 77:12

Being Together

There was a time when vacation trips and weekends were something for only a privileged and moneyed few. No longer.

Today there are all kinds of trips and tours and cruises especially geared to those who are getting on in years. Many travel abroad and see with their own eyes things and places they had read and heard about but never expected to see. I've heard that in Denmark retirement begins with a ten-day tour at company expense.

Travel is a remarkably enriching experience. It broadens our knowledge and expands our understanding of the world and its peoples. Travel—even if it is only to another section of our own city—opens our hearts and our minds. But most of all, best of all,

travel affords the opportunity for husband and wife to be together, to share something they will always and fondly remember.

Lord, it's wonderful to be able to go on an occasional trip or tour. But the best part is that we can do it together. Grant that we may share many glorious experiences together, and all that is yet to be.

So they are no longer two but one.

Matthew 19:6

Participation

Is youth all the world cares about? How about the rest of us, those of us who are getting on in years? Have we been forgotten? Have we been pushed aside?

As a matter of fact, No! Those of us who are getting on in years have a great deal going for us. Municipalities, public agencies, societies, churches—even business concerns—have gone to great lengths to sponsor activities, programs, and services especially for us. And then there are the host of "senior citizens" and "golden age" clubs run by and for people like us.

All that seems very dull and boring to younger people. But for those of us who are getting on in years these activities are a joy and a delight.

Quite apart from the activities themselves these groups and programs offer occasion for companionship and conviviality at our pace, and expanding circles of friendship at a stage in life when such circles are inevitably narrowing. The opportunity is there, to participate in what is going on if we will but take it.

Dear God, I am so grateful that I am not forgotten, that there are so many who care about those of us who are getting on in years. Thank you for the opportunity to participate in so much with so many.

This is the day which the Lord has made;
let us rejoice and be glad in it.

Psalm 118:24

Someone to Talk With

The men in this picture are getting on in years, well on. They meet almost every day as neighbors. Sometimes they pause at the fence or walk together a few blocks and then go their separate ways. Occasionally they may stop along the way and linger over a cup of coffee, or just spend an hour on a park bench, sharing yesterday's memories and today's chitchat.

But they enjoy each other's company. They feel comfortable with each other.

It's good to be at ease with others. Just to be with others, to talk with others—these are the stuff of which life and friendship are made. They keep the mind alive and alert, give us a new slant on things, help keep us in touch with life and with the world beyond our walls.

Getting on in years could mean a growing confinement in a world that grows ever smaller. But it can also mean enhanced opportunity to spend time in the company of others.

Thank you, God, for friends with whom I can converse, and with whom I can feel at ease. Help me to be the blessing to them that they are to me.

Hear, for I will speak noble things,
    and from my lips will come what is right.

Proverbs 8:6

Hidden Talent

Getting on in years? Why not take up a hobby! Especially if you have never had one.

It doesn't have to be the kind of hobby that produces something functional or saleable. The important thing is that you enjoy doing it.

Have fun! Read. Collect stamps, matchcovers, coins. Putter around at a workbench or in the garden (even if it is only a window box). Take up painting. Raise gerbils or goldfish.

Or write out the story of your life. Such a biography may be of more value and interest to those who come after you than you could ever suspect.

Who knows what hidden talent a hobby may bring to light?

But even if the hobby doesn't uncover hidden talent or genius, it can give you a great deal of pleasure. It can keep your mind keen and your hands active.

Lord, give me a hobby that will keep me alert and active, a hobby that will brighten my life and the lives of those around me.

I do not occupy myself with things
  too great and too marvelous for me.
But I have calmed and quieted my soul.

Psalm 131:1,2

Still Useful

Getting on in years? Of course you are. Everyone is.

But that doesn't mean you are ready for the scrap heap, that everything is behind you. Your best is yet to be given.

Strength and energy do not dry up and vanish overnight. Nor do the skills, talent, and ability developed, honed, and refined over a lifetime take flight upon retirement.

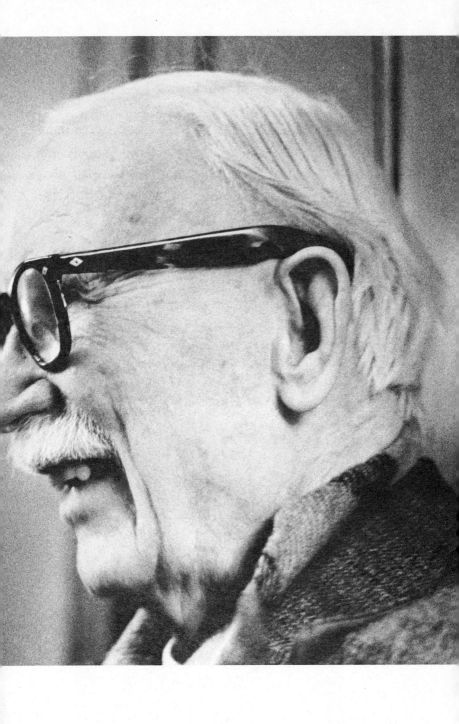

You know many things; you know how to do many things. You know them well; you know how to do them well. Others need your knowledge and skill, your talents and ability.

You are needed. Churches, service organizations, hospitals, homes, and institutions, even schools and business concerns need what you still have to give.

Don't let what you have go to waste. Put it to use. Don't hide your light under a bushel.

> Lord, I don't want to sit around and rust out. I want to use the knowledge and skills I've accumulated over the years. I want to show that I am still useful.

Nor do men light a lamp and put it under a bushel, but on a stand, and it gives light to all in the house.

Matthew 5:15

Remaining Silent

The ancient world held in high esteem those who were getting on in years. People sought and heeded their advice. Getting on in years does confer a certain kind of authority on us, doesn't it? Not the authority of power or of a sudden burst of wisdom, but the authority of experience.

To grow old means to have accumulated a great deal of experience, to have been through life's mill, to have made and profited from mistakes. That is the kind of experience no school can teach, no currency can buy. One acquires it only by getting on in years.

But we need not flaunt it. The great temptation of getting on in years is to want to pass that experience along in the form of gratuitous, unsolicited advice. Nothing is more likely to fall on deaf ears than such advice, however sound it may be.

One who is getting on in years successfully has learned when to keep his experience to himself, and to give advice only when asked.

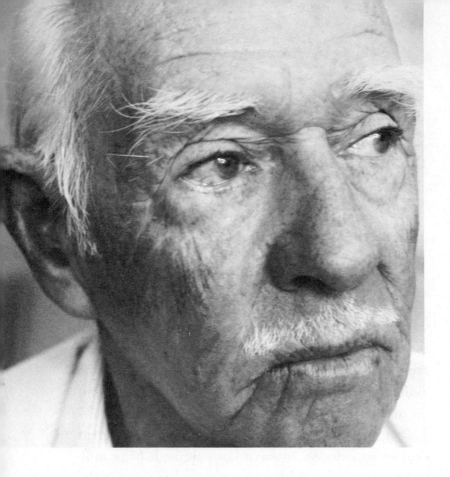

Heavenly Father, I know that I could help those younger than myself by giving them the benefit of my experience. Teach me from your own more ample experience and example that there is a time to offer advice and a time to remain silent.

For everything there is a season, and a time for every matter under heaven:
  a time to keep silence, and a time to speak.

Ecclesiastes 3:1, 7

Self-made
Loneliness

Being lonely and alone are the two things we dread most. Yet they come to us as we get on in years.

Infirmities catch up with us and we don't get around as we once did. Consequently we don't see as many of our relatives and old friends as we once did. Nor as often. They don't get around any better than we.

And then there is the inevitable. Death invades the circle of blood and friendship. We can scarcely bring ourselves to read the daily obituary list. The ringing of the phone at an unaccustomed hour fills us with apprehension that yet another has left us. Getting on in years means that death imposes loneliness and aloneness upon us.

But there is something far worse. Far worse is the loneliness we so often bring upon ourselves when we reject the friendly overtures of others who extend the heart and hand of friendship.

To be sure, they cannot replace those whom we have lost, those who shared our yesterday. But should we reject their willingness to share our today?

Lord, help me to respond in kind to those who reach out to me in my loneliness and aloneness.

If you have come to me in friendship to help me, my heart will be knit to you.

1 Chronicles 12:17

Making Concessions

It isn't only the candles on the birthday cake that tell us we are getting on in years. The aches and pains and ailments get the message across very effectively and often very painfully.

The foods we once enjoyed so much and from which we suffered no ill aftereffects are now mischief workers to our body. The desserts that once made and still make our mouths water are restricted or forbidden. The coffee we enjoyed so much, and probably too often, now robs us of our sleep and sets our nerves on edge.

We tire more quickly—and intensely—than in other years. We see the doctor far more frequently. At times it seems we take in more medicine than food.

We don't like any of this. Yet reason and good sense tell us we need to make concessions to our age. But

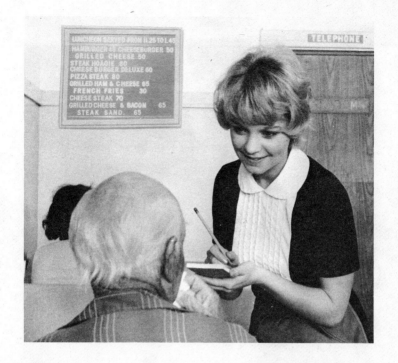

the right diet, moderate exercise, adequate rest, following our doctor's advice—these aren't just concessions to age. They are the accepting of God's provision for us as we get on in years.

> Lord, my body is a wonderful gift from you. Just as wonderful are the ways by which you help to keep it functioning as we get on in years. Help me to make the necessary concessions to age with thankful heart and joyful spirit.

My grace is sufficient for you, for my power is made perfect in weakness.

2 Corinthians 12:9

Self-Pity

"I'm getting on in years."

"My children neglect me."

"The neighbors are unfriendly."

"Why don't those noisy kids play somewhere else?"

"My back aches."

"My feet hurt."

"I can't get my rest, I don't sleep well at night."

"I can't eat right; nothing tastes anymore."

"No one cares what happens to me."

"They'll be sorry when I'm gone."

Sound familiar? Perhaps you haven't said it in these words. But you have complained, often without real cause. The truth of the matter is that you are feeling sorry for yourself.

All of us have those moments. But we must keep them at the barest minimum. Self-pity alienates us from those around us. Self-pity sends a poison through our being that is more deadly than any disease. Self-pity is a thief that robs us of the joy and peace God sends each day.

> O God, I don't want to feel sorry for myself. I don't want to complain. Help me to rejoice and be thankful for each day's blessings, and for those that are yet to be.

My soul melts away for sorrow;
strengthen me according to thy word!

Psalm 119:28

Forgiveness

Life offers us more opportunities than we can count or recognize—not all of them good. One is the opportunity to quarrel with a friend.

A word spoken one way is understood in another. Some act or gesture is misunderstood. Perhaps a jest is carried too far and gets out of hand.

Then faces flush with anger. Feelings become raw. Harsh and ugly words dart from our mouths.

To be sure, no blood is shed; no violence is done. But in a matter of moments lifelong friendships are shattered and broken.

Then comes the regret. As we get on in years we recognize the things we are sorry about.

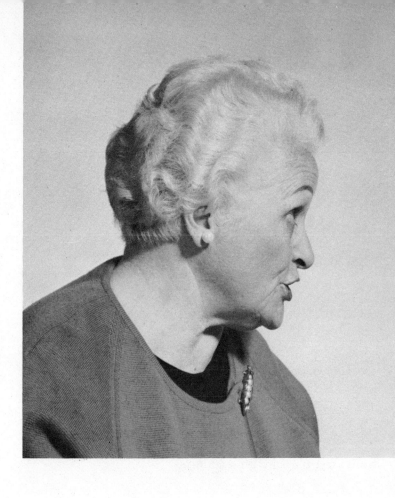

Most of all we regret that we have harbored and nurtured feelings of anger and bitterness toward others who once were friends. In many instances we see—often reluctantly—that we were at fault.

However long life may be, it is too short to bear grudges, to harbor feelings of anger or guilt. It is best for us to forgive, and to ask forgiveness—now, while there is still time.

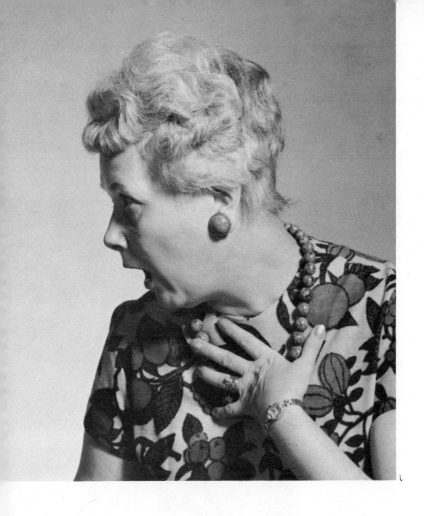

Lord, give me the courage and the will to forgive those who have wronged me, and to seek the pardon of those whom I have wronged.

Be kind to one another, tenderhearted, forgiving one another, as God in Christ forgave you.

Ephesians 4:32

To Love and to Cherish

" . . . to love and to cherish, till death us do part."
Once we pledged to each other our lives, our total
selves, at the marriage altar. We meant every word of
it. We still mean it.

But pledges often meet with default. The truth is
that we have not always loved and cherished each
other. We have used and abused each other shame-
fully. We have taken out on each other the hurt, anger,
and frustration against which we could not strike
back in any other way. We have blamed each other
for our own failures and inadequacies.

We have made molehills into mountains and dwelt
at length and without respite upon each other's faults
and flaws. We have done and said things which pained
and wounded. Even long years afterwards the pain
still aches, and the wound still bleeds.

Certainly it is good and necessary to forgive those
who have wronged us, and to be forgiven by those
whom we have wronged. Even more important is it
to forgive and be forgiven right away, especially
at home, to exchange forgiveness at once with the one
to whom we once made the pledge " . . . till death us
do part."

Help us to forgive each other, O Lord. Help us
to heal each other's wounds.

*Be angry but do not sin; do not let the sun go down on
your anger.*

Ephesians 4:26

Closer to God

There are always those who out of ignorance or hostility to the church revive an old slander. They say the church is dying, that only the aged care about religion. The day is coming, they say, when the church and those who adhere to it will belong only to the past—they will be buried together in the tomb of ancient history.

It is not necessary to refute that slander here, suffice it to say that the church is still here, while its detractors have gone—and will go—the way of all flesh.

With age, though, awareness of God grows. That is true. As we get on in years we become more aware of God than ever before.

Faced by the ultimate of life, we yearn for the promised best that is yet to be. We seek better to know and understand—and come to terms with—what lies beyond life and death. No, not *what* lies beyond life and death but *who* is there to meet us.

And so we are more conscientious about church-going. We want to hear God's word, receive the pledges offered in the Lord's Supper, and share in the life of God's family, the church. In short, we want to draw closer to God, and we find as we attempt to do so that he has already drawn closer to us.

> Dear Lord, I thank you for the church. Through it I can draw close to you and know that you have drawn close to me.

I was glad when they said unto me, "Let us go into the house of the Lord!"

Psalm 122:1

Anniversary

Life together! For so many years! Just think of it!
Where did the years all go? It doesn't seem all that
long ago.

And think of all that's happened in those years!
The sweat, the tears, the fears. The smiles and laughs
and little triumphs.

And see how it all turned out! Things didn't
always turn out the way we expected or planned or
hoped. But they did turn out—and much better than
seemed possible at the time.

Looking back on the succession of years, we remember the words spoken at our marriage:

> "And although, by reason of sin, many a cross hath been laid thereon, nonetheless our heavenly Father doth not forsake those in an estate so pleasing to him, but is ever present with his abundant blessings."

Indeed he has been present. And he has blessed and kept, preserved and healed, in more ways than we recognized.

We see now what then we did not even faintly suspect: there is always more to come, more and better than we could ever imagine.

> We thank you, Lord, for our years together. We also thank you for the years that may be left to us, for they too will be under your protection and blessing.

> *He has said, "I will never fail you nor forsake you."*
> *Hebrews 13:5*

Newspaper and Bible

There was a time when people read the Bible not just once in a while but regularly, daily. The day began and ended with the Bible. Nowadays the day begins and ends with the newspaper.

But Bible and newspaper belong together. The newspaper tells us what is happening in the world, invariably the worst. The Bible enables us to understand what the newspaper reports, and to hope for the best. The newspaper illustrates over and over in contemporary and concrete terms our need for the message the Bible brings.

The more we get on in years the more confusing the world becomes to us. The times seem so out of joint. Things get out of focus and perspective. The Bible helps us to see things in focus and perspective.

By all means read the newspaper. But remember to read—learn, mark, and inwardly digest—the Bible.

> "O may these heavenly pages be
> My ever dear delight . . .
> Teach me to love thy sacred word
> And view my Saviour there."
> —Anne Steele, 1716-78

All scripture is inspired by God and profitable for teaching, for reproof, for correction, and for training in righteousness, that the man of God may be complete, equipped for every good work.

2 Timothy 3:16,17

Dying

Even though I walk through the valley of the shadow of death, I fear no evil; for thou art with me.

Psalm 23:4

Getting on in years? So are scores of millions of others.

Medical science has made incredible advances. Illnesses that once meant certain death have been overcome. Miracle drugs and sophisticated surgical techniques and equipment have made it possible for more and more of us to get farther on in years than ever before, and at the same time to enjoy reasonably good health.

Death can now be staved off longer—but not forever. Everyone must die. Yes, even we must die. We must learn to live with that fact.

Even more important is it to learn to live *and* die with him who is the Lord over death and the giver of life. All things are in his hands: birth and death, beginning and end, yesterday and tomorrow. Our lives are hidden in him who is the fulfiller of all things, the giver of all that is yet to be.

> Help me, Lord, to live each day as though it were
> my last, not in fear and trembling, but in the joy
> and confidence that springs from faith in you.

And After Death, Life!

Is there really life after death, a heavenly kingdom where the "former things have passed away," where "God will wipe away every tear"?

Or is that just an idle tale, a story for children—like those "happily ever after" stories—something to make the pain of living bearable?

Can we really believe that there on the other side of death, waiting for the billions who have lived on this earth and waiting especially for us, is the Lord himself? Yes, we can and do believe. Yes, the best is yet to be!

And the farther we get on in years ourselves the more certain we become. It is we, not just those people of long ago, for whom Jesus Christ came into the world, gave his life on the cross, and was raised from the dead.

What proof do we have for this belief, what hard, solid proof? None but the faith to which God bears witness in our hearts and minds, constant and unwavering witness. And that's enough for us, more than enough.

Death is not the end. Death is the beginning— of Life!

Dear Lord, there have been times when I have doubted and denied what my heart knows is true. Even now there are moments when my faith and trust waver. But not for long. When I look to Jesus, the doubts are gone.

I know whom I have believed and I am sure that he is able to guard until that Day what has been entrusted to me.

2 Timothy 1:12

My times are in thy hand.
Psalm 21:15